Introduction

Have you ever wondered what lies in space beyond the comfort of our planet? There is a whole family of planets in the Solar System, many with their own moons.

This book will take you off into space, to explore Mercury and Venus, stopping at Earth and our Moon, and then on to Mars, Jupiter, Saturn, Uranus, Neptune and Pluto. Discover the amazing moons that orbit these planets and learn about other features found in the Solar System such as asteroids, comets and meteoroids.

• In this book, a billion is one thousand million.

Spot and count!

Q: Why watch out for these boxes?

A: They give answers to the space questions you always wanted to ask.

Space bits

Look out for these boxes to take a closer look at space features.

Awesome facts

Watch out for these diamonds to learn more about the truly weird and wonderful facts about the planets and their moons.

Scientists have worked out that the Solar System formed 4,560 million years ago. At first, it was just a dark whirling mass of gas and dust. But as it spun, gravity pulled bits tighter together. The dense centre became the Sun, and dust further out came together to form the planets.

Earth

Venu

Sun

Mercury

The Solar System

The Earth doesn't just hang in space. It zooms at the amazing speed of almost 107,000 km/h around the Sun. Earth isn't alone. Another eight huge balls, called planets, circle around the Sun too – all held in place by the pull of the Sun's gravity. The Sun and all its circling companions are together called the Solar System.

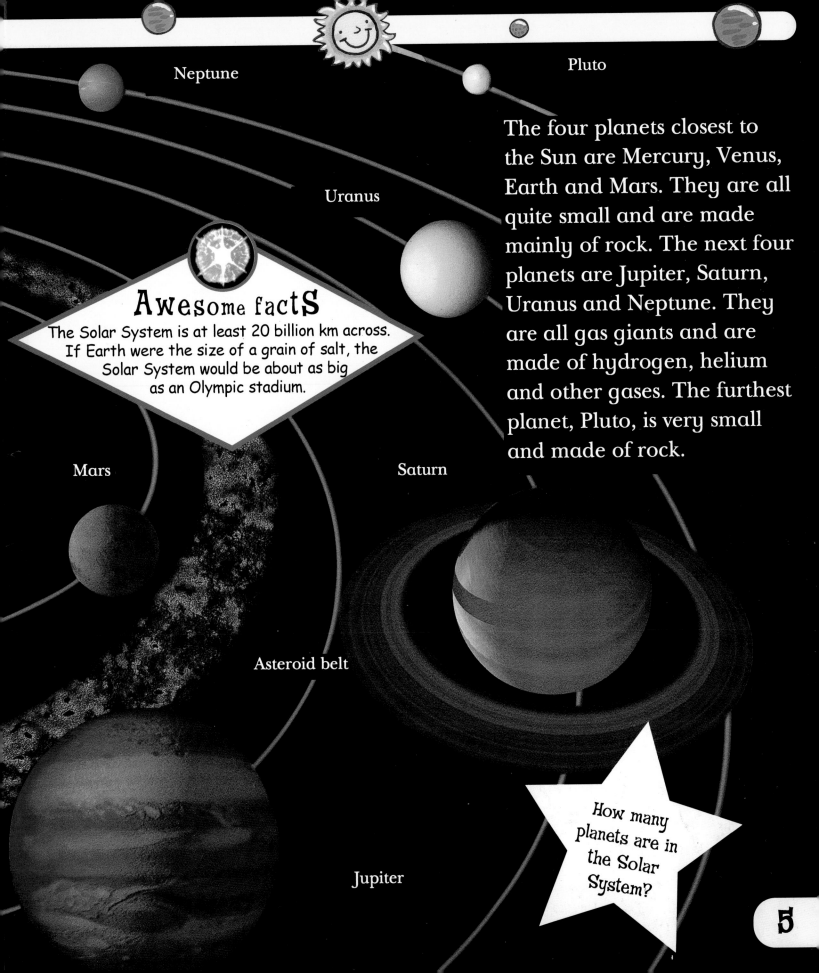

Neptune

Pluto

Uranus

The four planets closest to the Sun are Mercury, Venus, Earth and Mars. They are all quite small and are made mainly of rock. The next four planets are Jupiter, Saturn, Uranus and Neptune. They are all gas giants and are made of hydrogen, helium and other gases. The furthest planet, Pluto, is very small and made of rock.

Awesome factS

The Solar System is at least 20 billion km across. If Earth were the size of a grain of salt, the Solar System would be about as big as an Olympic stadium.

Mars

Saturn

Asteroid belt

How many planets are in the Solar System?

Jupiter

5

zoom in on...

Mercury's surface

Mercury is small, so its gravity is weak and can't hold onto an atmosphere. There is nothing to protect the planet from the Sun's rays or stop meteors bashing into it. So it is even more deeply dented with craters than the Moon. A journey across the surface would show you nothing more than vast, empty basins, cliffs hundreds of kilometres long and yellow dust everywhere.

Earth

Mercury

Mercury is smaller than some of Jupiter's moons. It is 20 times lighter than the Earth and barely a third of the diameter.

 Q: If Mercury takes 59 days to turn round, how come the Sun stays up for 176 days?

A: Mercury rotates slowly, but whizzes round the Sun in just 88 days (compared to 365 days for the Earth). This means that as it turns slowly away from the Sun, it whizzes round the other side so that the sunny side is still facing the Sun.

Mercury

Mercury is the nearest planet to the Sun, often less than 58 million km away. Mercury has little atmosphere to protect it, so the side facing the Sun is scorched (up to 430°C), while the dark side is icy cold (-180°C).

Earth turns round once on its axis in 23 hours 56 minutes. Mercury takes nearly 59 Earth days to turn once round its axis.

Mercury

Every so often, Mercury passes across the face of the Sun when seen from the Earth.

Like Earth, Mercury has polar ice caps – but the ice is made from acid!

Venus

Venus is almost exactly the same size as the Earth. It measures about 12,000 km across and weighs just a little less than the Earth. It is sometimes called the Evening Star or the Morning Star. This is because it is quite close to the Sun, so it can be seen in the night sky just after sunset and just before sunrise.

zoom in on...

Atmosphere

Venus is a beautiful planet covered in swirls of pinky white cloud. But the pink clouds are actually made partly of sulphuric acid. They are so thick that they press down on the planet's surface hard enough to crush a car!

Venus

Moon

When Our Moon is a new crescent moon, it is between the Earth and the Sun. Venus lies between the Earth and the Sun too. So sometimes you will see Venus near the new Moon as it rises.

The surface of Venus can't be seen since it is hidden behind swirls of pinky white cloud. It was probably once covered in huge oceans, but they all boiled away. All that is left are just hot, bone-dry, rolling plains dotted with volcanoes and vast plateaux such as Lakshmi Plateau.

Computer reconstruction of Venus's surface

Awesome facts

Huge amounts of carbon dioxide in Venus's atmosphere trap heat on the surface and boost temperatures to a scorching 470°C, the hottest in the Solar System.

Planet Earth

Earth is the third planet out from the Sun, about 150 million km away. It is not so close to the Sun that it is scorching hot, nor so far away that it is icy cold. It has water on its surface, and can sustain life.

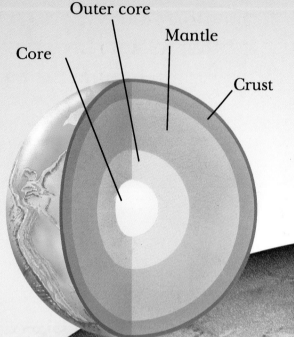

Core

Outer core

Mantle

Crust

Q: Why can we live on our planet?

A: Earth is a special place. It is the only planet we know that has water on its surface, and water makes life possible. It also has a blanket of gases, called the atmosphere, which we breathe.

The Earth is made mostly of rock and is the densest planet in the Solar System. But it is not just a solid ball. It has a shell or crust of hard rock. Beneath that is a layer almost 3,000 km deep of warm partly melted rock, called the mantle. The centre is a core made entirely of hot metal, mostly iron.

zoom in on...

Earth is not round!

The Earth is not quite round. The way the Earth spins makes it bulge out at the middle, round the equator. The Earth is 43 km narrower between the poles than around the equator.

The Earth whizzes once around the Sun every year. It is slightly tilted over. So as it travels round the Sun, the zone on Earth nearest the Sun gradually shifts. This is what creates seasons – the part of the world nearest the Sun has summer, the part which is farthest away has winter. The equator has no seasons.

70% of the Earth is ocean. Can you spot the land?

Our Moon

The Moon is Earth's companion. It is 384,400 km away, but that is very, very close in space terms. In fact, the Moon circles round the Earth about once a month – which is how we got the word 'month' (or 'moonth').

The Moon seems to change shape over a month. We only see the side of the Moon that is lit by the Sun. As the Moon circles the Earth, we see it from different angles – and so see more or less of its sunlit side.

At the new moon (1), we see a thin crescent-shaped sliver. This grows over the next two weeks to a full moon (3), when we see all the sunlit side. It then shrinks back over the rest of the month to a crescent-shape – the old moon (5).

1

2

3

4

5

The Moon is a barren lifeless place covered with dust and craters caused by huge lumps of rock crashing into it billions of years ago, when the Moon was young.

Q: How was the Moon made?

A: Amazingly, the Moon was probably made by a space collision. About 4,500 million years ago, soon after the Earth formed, a planet at least as big as Mars collided with Earth. The crash completely melted the other planet and splashes flew off into space. Gradually, gravity pulled these splashes together into a ball which cooled to form the Moon.

A large object hits the Earth. The object melts and splashes of debris fly into space.

Debris spins in orbit and joins together to form the Moon.

Awesome facts

There are huge dark patches on the Moon called seas which have never had a drop of water. They are plains formed long ago by hot molten rock from the Moon's inside.

Craters on
Mars's surface

zoom in on...

Water on Mars?

In the 1880s, astronomers
thought dark lines they saw on
Mars's surface were actually canals built
by Martians. They proved to be optical
illusions, but valleys show water once
flowed over the surface in abundance.

Valley on
Mars's surface

Ice-covered pole

Mars

Mars is the only planet to have an atmosphere or daytime temperatures anything like ours. But Mars is a desert planet, with no oceans or any sign of life – just red rocks and dust and a pink sky.

 Q: Are there any volcanoes on Mars?

A: Like Earth and Venus, Mars has volcanoes. In fact, Olympus Mons (below) on Mars is the biggest volcano in the Solar System – three times higher than Mount Everest!

More spacecraft have landed on Mars than on any planet. In 1997, the Mars Pathfinder landed and sent out a robot truck to scan the area and beam back TV pictures. In the near future, missions to Mars hope to probe beneath the surface to search for signs of microscopic life.

Asteroid

Comet

Meteorite

A meteoroid is dirt and debris from an asteroid or comet. It can be seen as a meteor as it burns in Earth's atmosphere. If it reaches Earth, usually no bigger than a lump of coal, it is called a meteorite. Comets are like huge dirty snowballs in the outer reaches of the Solar System. A comet's core is just a few kilometres across, but when it swings in close to the Sun and partly melts, it throws out a vast glistening tail of dust and gas.

Asteroids, comets and meteoroids

There are hundreds of thousands of tiny pieces of rock and ice whizzing round the Sun, including asteroids, comets and meteoroids. Some are no bigger than sultanas, but the biggest asteroid, Ceres, is 933 km across. Two asteroids even have their own moons.

Halley's comet is visible for several weeks every 76 years or so.

The Meteor Crater in Arizona is a vast bowl that formed when a meteorite crashed into the Arizona desert 50,000 years ago. The impact created a hole over 1,200 m across and 200 m deep.

?

Q: Where are most asteroids found?

A: Most asteroids circle the Sun in a huge band between Mars and Jupiter called the asteroid belt. It may be the last remnants of a smashed planet. There are 26 asteroids that are over 200 km across, over a million that are at least 1 km across and billions of smaller bits!

Jupiter

Asteroid belt

Sun

Mars

17

Jupiter's gravity is so powerful that it squeezes hydrogen and helium gases until they become liquid or solid. Under the thin atmosphere is an ocean of liquid hydrogen and a small rocky core.

Jupiter weighs 318 times as much as the Earth. Its colourful clouds are whipped into long belts by violent winds, which blow at up to 500 km/h.

Awesome facts

Jupiter turns right round in under 10 hours, compared to 24 hours for Earth. At Jupiter's equator, the surface is whizzing round at over 47,000 km/h!

Jupiter

Jupiter is gigantic. It is by far the biggest planet in the Solar System – over 140,000 km across – and it takes 12 years to go round the Sun. It is a huge ball of gas, more like the Sun than the Earth, and is made mostly of hydrogen and helium. You can see it clearly for part of the year. It is brighter than any of the stars.

Find the Great Red Spot.

Q: What is the red spot?

A: The Great Red Spot, or GRS, is a dark red swirl of clouds in Jupiter's atmosphere first noticed over 300 years ago. It seems to be a gigantic hurricane, with very strong winds.

If you were on Ganymede you would see Jupiter in the sky.

Jupiter's moons

Jupiter has at least 16 moons. The four largest (Io, Europa, Ganymede and Callisto) were discovered by a scientist called Galileo in 1610. Ganymede and Callisto are larger than our own Moon, and the other two are not much smaller.

Ganymede

Awesome facts

Jupiter has 16 known moons but there may be others too small to have been seen yet. You can see the four biggest moons with an ordinary pair of binoculars!

Until Galileo saw through his telescope that Jupiter's moons circled round it, people thought that everything in the Universe circled round the Earth.

zoom in on...

Europa's oceans

Europa has a very bright, smooth surface of ice with liquid water beneath. Scientists think that there might be life forms in this water. In places the surface of Europa is cracked like an egg shell.

Europa

Callisto

Io

Io has been called the most volcanic body in the Solar System. When the Voyager 2 space probe passed it in 1979, it discovered that plumes of material were being shot out from Io's surface up to a height of 300 km. It was the first evidence of active volcanoes anywhere other than the Earth.

21

Changing rings

1995

2000

2005

2009

2011

Awesome facts

The temperature of Saturn's rocky core is about twice as hot as the surface temperature of the Sun.

We see Saturn at different angles at different times so we can see Saturn's rings better sometimes than others. In 1995, the rings were edge on and hard to see. In 2005, they will be at a greater angle, giving us a clear view.

Saturn

Saturn is the second largest planet, a gas giant over 120,000 km across. Around it circle not only an amazing halo of rings stretching out 70,000 km, but also, beyond the rings, at least 22 moons – more than any other planet.

 Q: What are Saturn's rings made of?

A: Saturn's rings are bands of countless billions of tiny blocks of ice and dust, circling the planet endlessly. Each ring is thousands of kilometres wide.

Uranus

Uranus is so far from the Sun that temperatures on its surface drop to -210°C. In this amazing cold, the methane (natural gas) that covers the planet turns to liquid oceans thousands of kilometres deep. It is these icy oceans that give Uranus its beautiful blue colour.

Uranus tilts so far over that it's on its side. It spins round once every 17 hours, but this has no effect on the length of a day. Instead, the day depends on where Uranus is in its orbit. When the south pole is pointing directly at the Sun, the Sun doesn't go down there for 20 years!

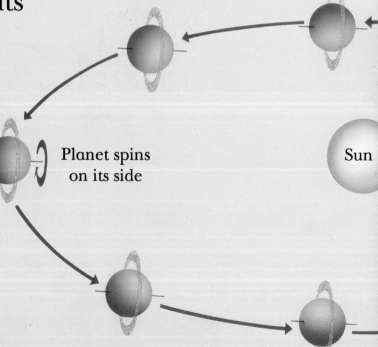

Planet spins on its side

Sun

Awesome facts

Because Uranus rolls round the Sun on its side, the Sun does some odd things. In spring, the Sun rises and sets every nine hours – backwards!

Uranus's icy atmosphere is made of hydrogen and helium. Winds whistle through it at over 2,000 km/h, ten times faster than the fastest hurricane on Earth. If you fell into its icy oceans for even a fraction of a second, you'd freeze so hard you could be shattered like glass.

Uranus's moon, Oberon

Long year

Uranus is almost three billion kilometres from the Sun. This far out, the distance Uranus has to travel round the Sun is vast – and takes over 84 Earth years. So on Uranus, you'd be collecting your pension on your first birthday.

Neptune

Neptune is the fourth largest planet in the Solar System. It's so far from the Sun – about 4.5 billion km – that it takes 164.79 years to go round the Sun. Indeed, it hasn't even gone right round once since it was first discovered back in 1846.

Cloud features on Neptune's surface

zoom in on...

Scooter

Neptune has raging storms and clouds on its surface that come and go over the years, probably driven by Neptune's internal heat. It also has a small white cloud of methane ice crystals that zips round the planet once every 16 hours and so is now known as the Scooter.

Great Dark Spot appears on different places on Neptune's surface.

26

Awesome factS

Neptune is the windiest place in the Solar System, with winds of over 2,500 km/h! You could throw a paper dart faster than the fastest jet plane.

Neptune is an icy blue planet like Uranus, covered in oceans of liquid methane. Surface temperatures on Neptune plunge to -210°C – but its moon Triton is even colder, with temperatures a chilling 236°C below zero. Triton's surface is covered in volcanoes that erupt – ice!

Triton

Surface of Triton

Can you spot the clouds on Neptune's surface?

27

Pluto

Pluto is the most remote planet in the Solar System – a tiny, lonely world smaller than our Moon. It is so far from the Sun that the Sun looks little bigger than a star in the sky and shines no brighter than the Moon. Sunlight only takes eight minutes to reach Earth, but takes up to six hours to reach Pluto.

Pluto has a moon almost half its size, called Charon. Pluto and Charon circle round each other, locked together in space like a pair of weightlifter's dumbbells. So Charon always stays in the same place in Pluto's sky, looking three times as big as our Moon.

Q: How big is Pluto compared to Earth?

A: Pluto is only 2,274 km across – barely a fifth of the size of Earth. Because it is so small and hard to spot Pluto was only discovered in 1930.

Pluto

Earth

zoom in on...

Charlene!

The man who found Charon in 1978 was going to call it after his wife Charlene. But he chose Charon after the ferryman who took lost souls to the Greek underworld, land of Pluto.

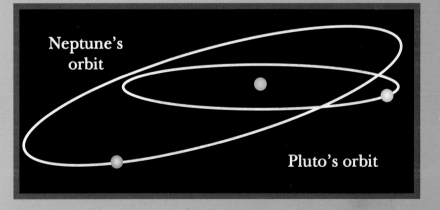

Neptune's orbit

Pluto's orbit

Pluto has an odd oval orbit. Most of the time, it is billions of kilometres out beyond Neptune. But for several years every three centuries, it actually moves in closer to the Sun than Neptune.

29

Planet facts

Use the table below to help you compare some fascinating facts about the nine planets in our Solar System. Use the illustration (*below*) to remind you of their order.

PLANET	NO. OF MOONS	MASS X EARTH	DISTANCE FROM SUN (MILLIONS OF KILOMETRES)	LENGTH OF YEAR
Mercury	0	0.055	58	88 days
Venus	0	0.82	108	225 days
Earth	1	1.00	150	365.25 days
Mars	2	0.11	228	687 days
Jupiter	16	317.8	778	11.9 years
Saturn	22	95.2	1,432	29.5 years
Uranus	15	14.5	2,871	84.1 years
Neptune	8	17.2	4,498	164.9 years
Pluto	1	0.002	5,914	248 years

Glossary

Asteroids
Small, rocky objects, the greatest collection of which orbit the Sun in a band called the asteroid belt, between Mars and Jupiter.

Atmosphere
The layer of gases that surrounds a planet. The atmosphere around the Earth supplies us with the oxygen that keeps us alive.

Comets
Lumps of ice and dust that orbit the Sun. As a comet approaches the Sun, heat from the Sun causes the ice and dust to boil off, creating huge tails that stretch out behind the comet.

Crater
A bowl-shaped pit on the surface of a planet. Some are caused by volcanoes, and some by the impact of a meteorite.

Equator
An imaginary line that runs around the middle of a planet at an equal distance from its two poles.

Gravity
Every object in the Universe has a force that attracts it to every other object. This force is called gravity. The Solar System is held together by the Sun's gravitational pull.

Great Red Spot
A dark red swirl of clouds in Jupiter's atmosphere.

Meteorite
A meteor that hits the Earth's surface.

Meteoroids
Small pieces of space debris which orbit the Sun.

Meteors
Objects that hit the Earth's atmosphere and burn up leaving a fiery tail that disappears after a few seconds.

Moons
Small bodies that orbit around some of the major planets. Earth has one moon, while Venus has none and Jupiter has 16.

Orbit
The path of an object, such as a planet or a comet, around another object, such as a star.

Planets
Large objects that orbit around a star. These can be rocky planets such as the Earth, Venus or Mars, or gassy giant planets, such as Jupiter, Saturn or Uranus.

Pole
A point on a planet's surface around which the planet spins or rotates.

Solar System
The group of major planets, including Earth, and minor planets that orbit the Sun.

Index

Picture credits
Abbreviations: t-top, m-middle, b-bottom, r-right, l-left
All photographs supplied by Stockbyte except for
Cover main, 1b, 10bl, 12tr, 12-13, 15br, 17tl, 18ml, 18-19, 20t, 21bl, 22-23, 24-25, 27br — Corbis.